Zen Elephant

The Art of Gratitude

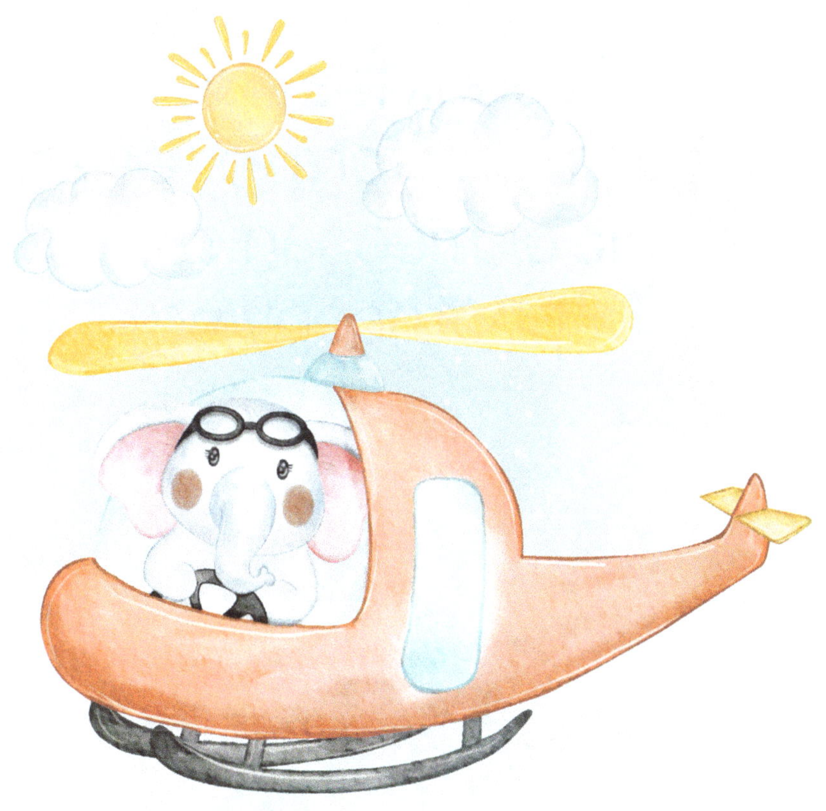

ISBN: 979-8-9886895-3-9
Copyright © 2023 by Jonathan Hill
All rights reserved.
No part of this book may be reproduced or transmitted in any form or by any means, electronic or mechanical, including photocopying

This Book Belongs to

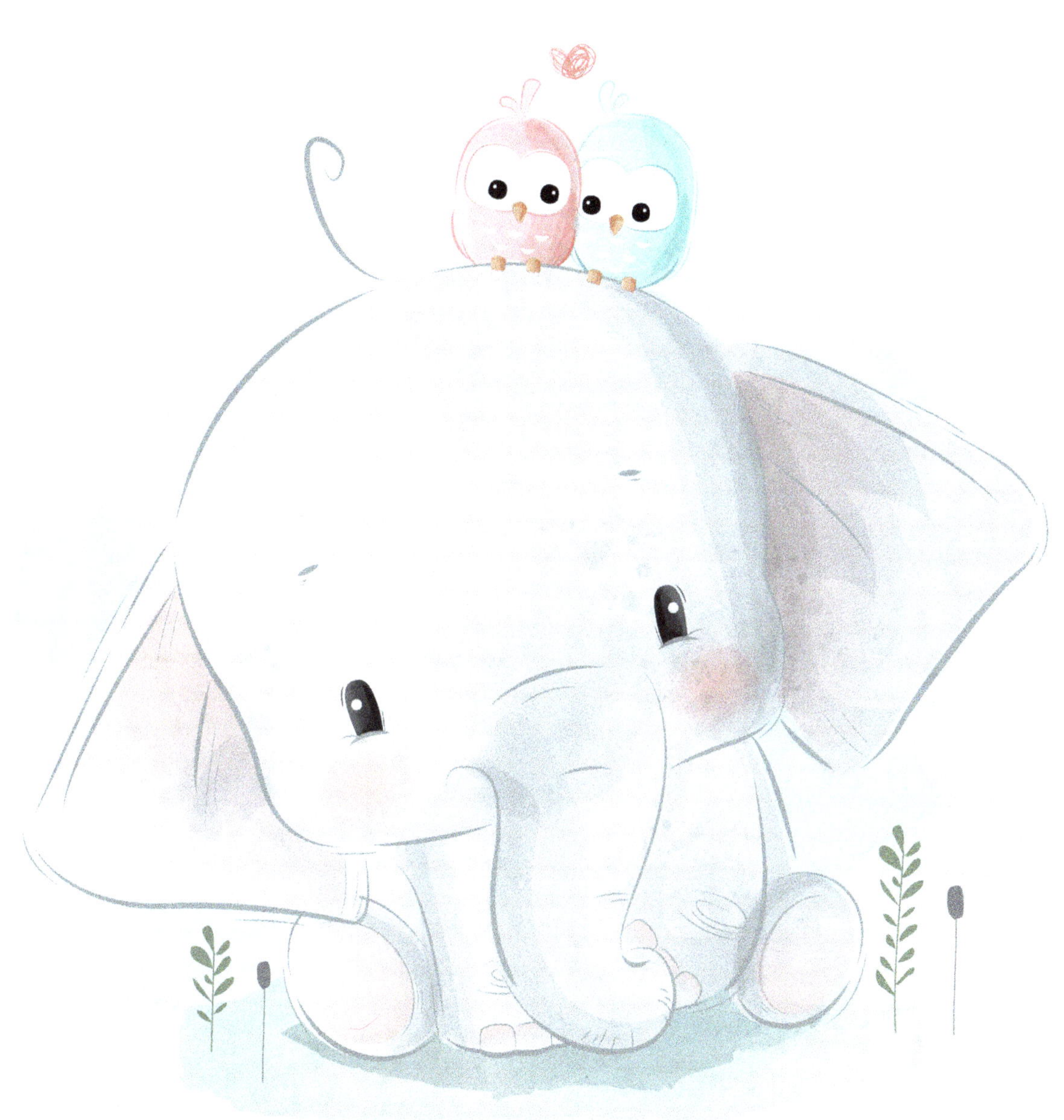

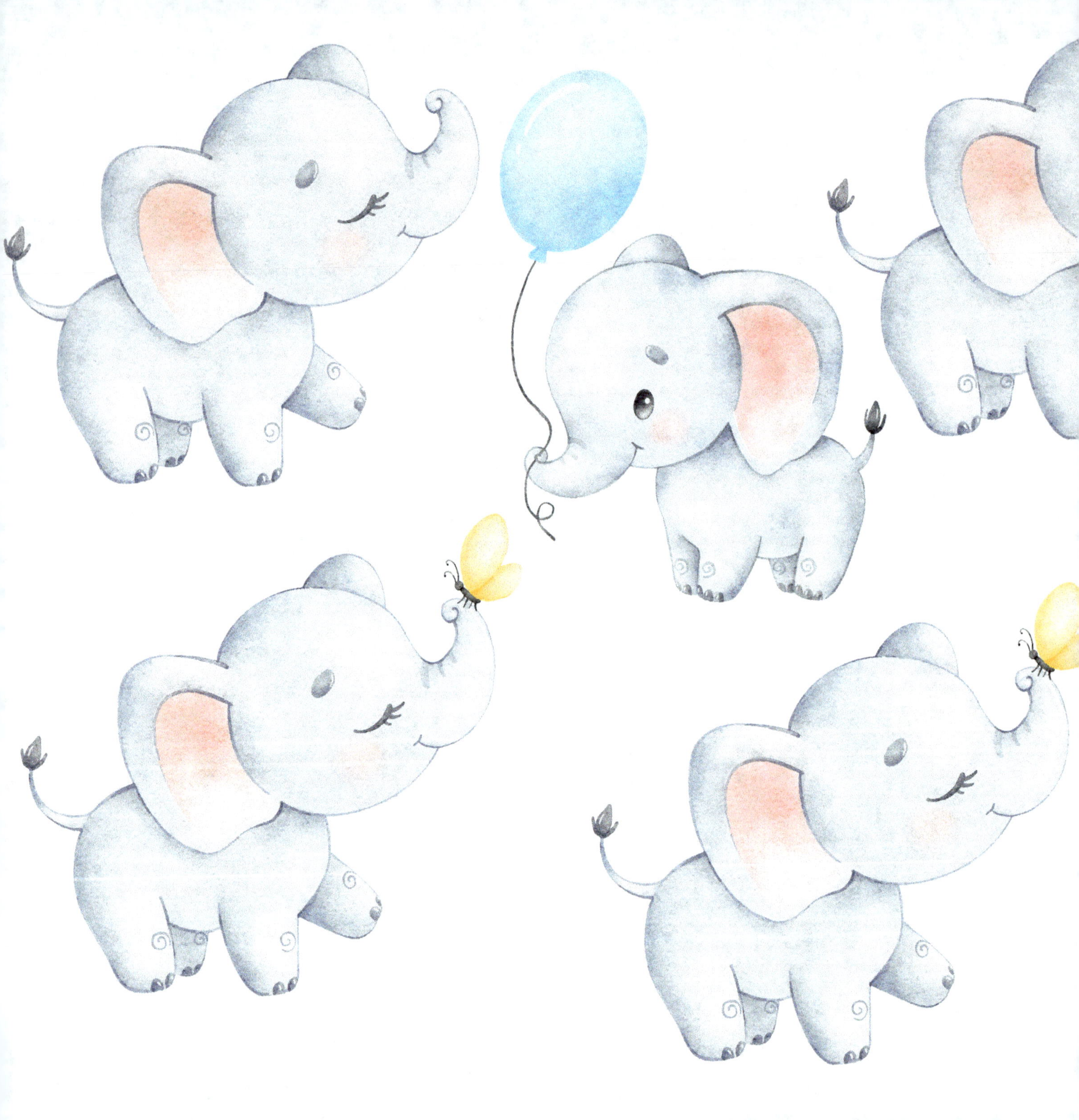

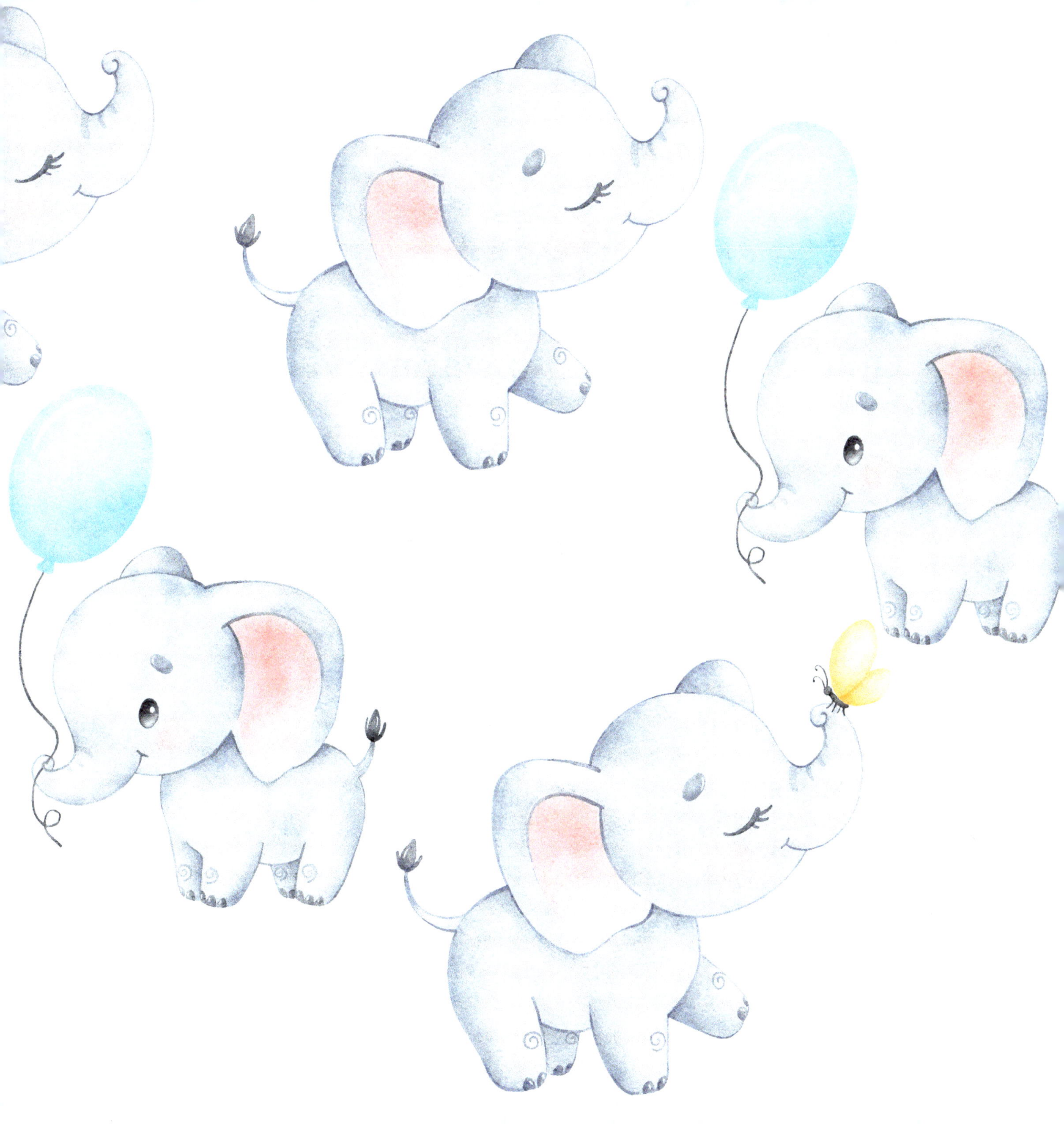

On the golden sun, so warm and bright,

Zen Elephant meditates,

embracing the light.

"Each new day," he softly sighs,

"Is a gift, a wonderful surprise."

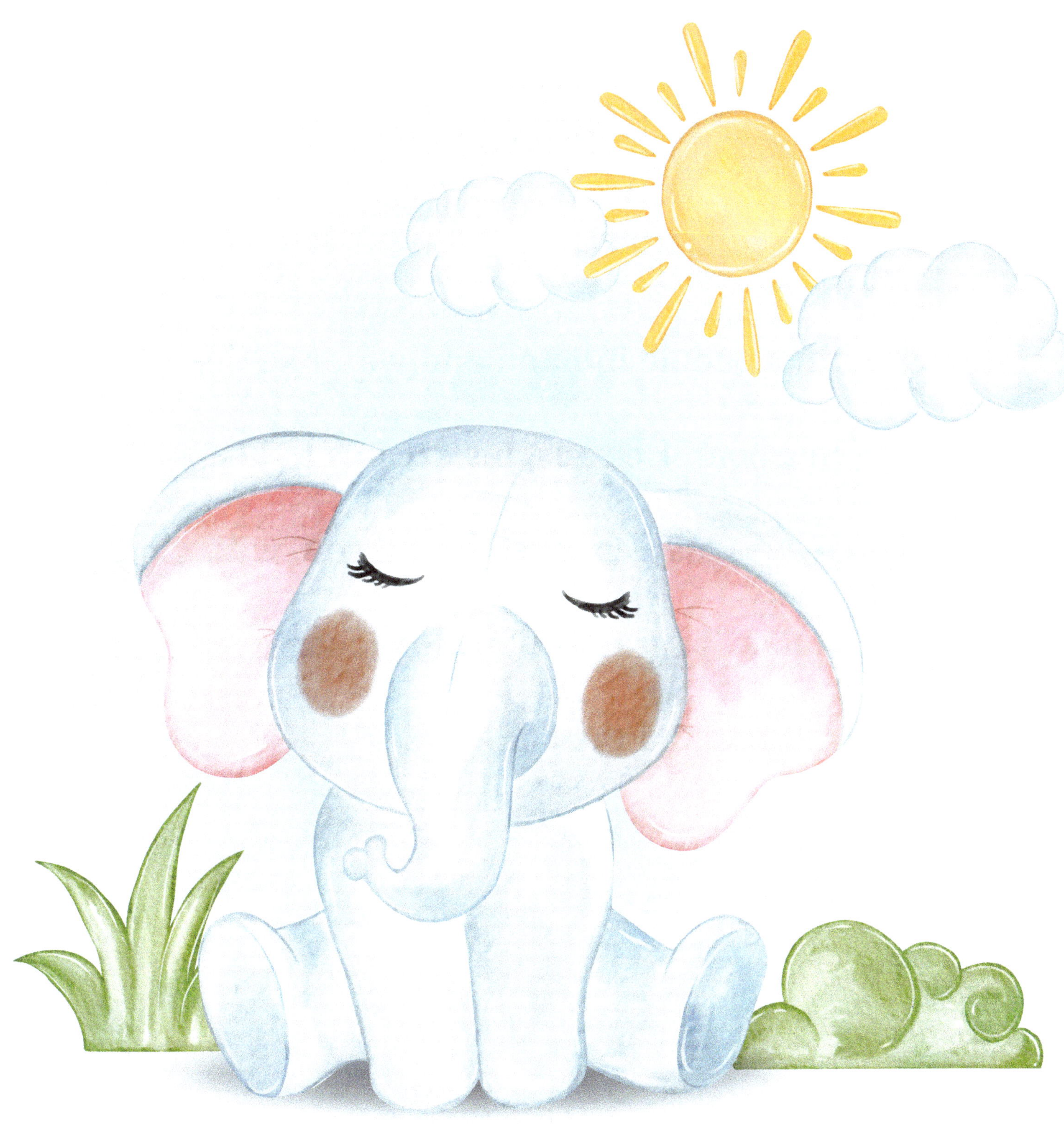

With a paddle in hand and water so deep,

On a boat, He sails, his dreams to keep.

"The waves may change, but I'll row with glee,

For I'm grateful for this journey,

and the endless sea."

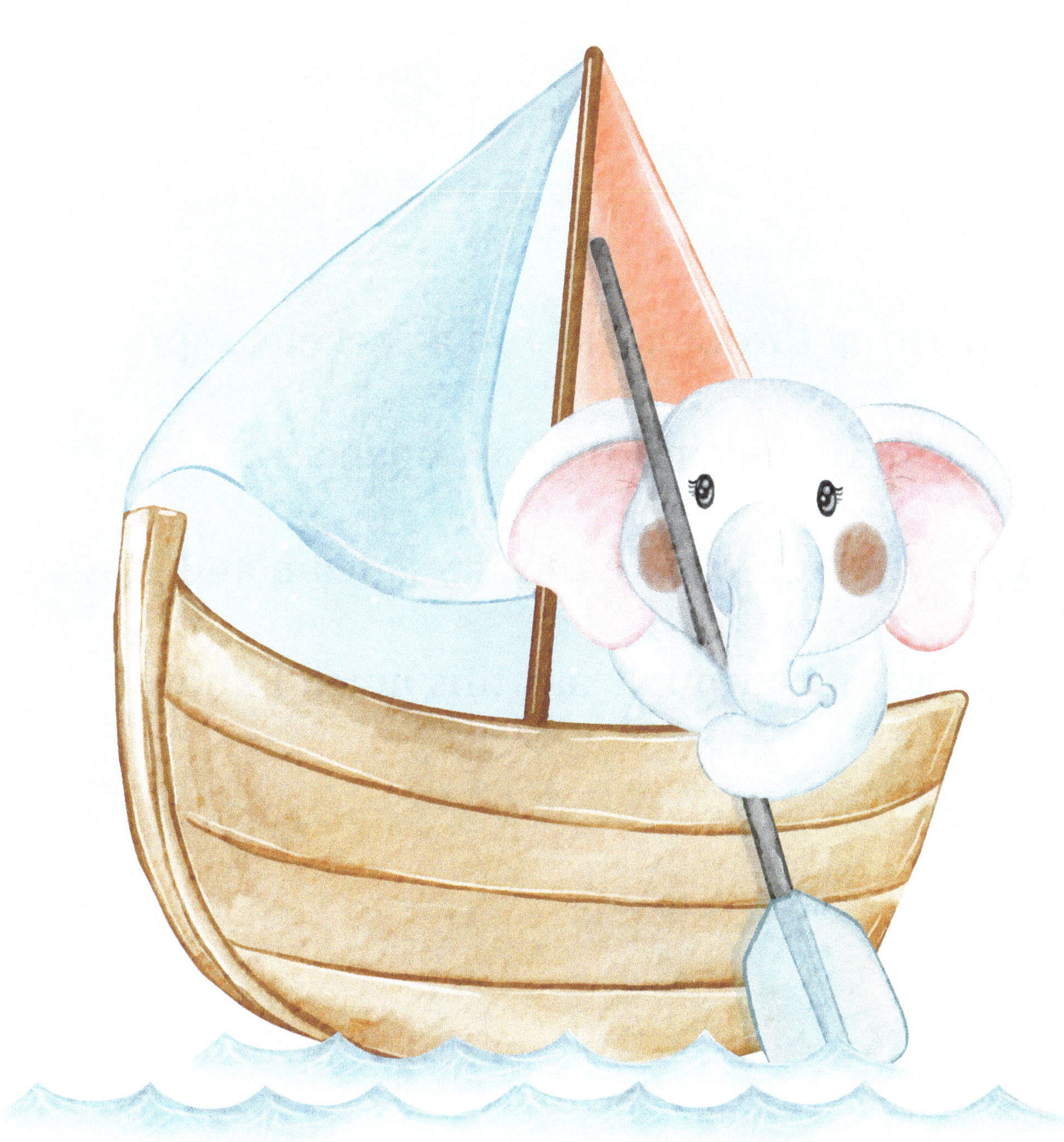

Blasting through stars on a rocket so spry,

He touches the vast open sky.

"Even up high, where the stars gleam and glow,

Gratitude grounds me, this much I know."

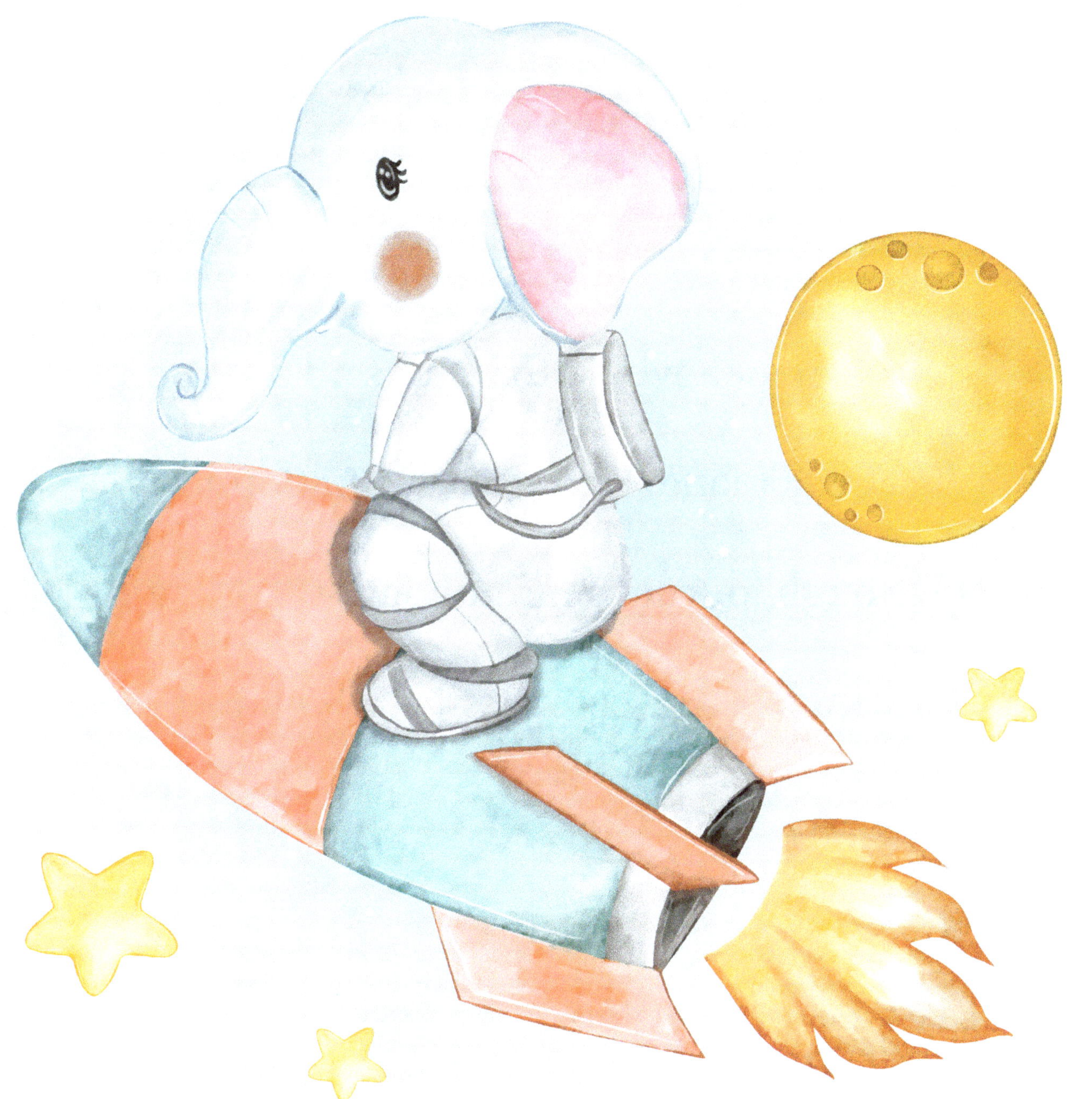

Soaring above, with clouds all around,

On a plane, He feels love unbound.

"Through journeys far and landscapes wide,

Gratitude is the compass by which I abide."

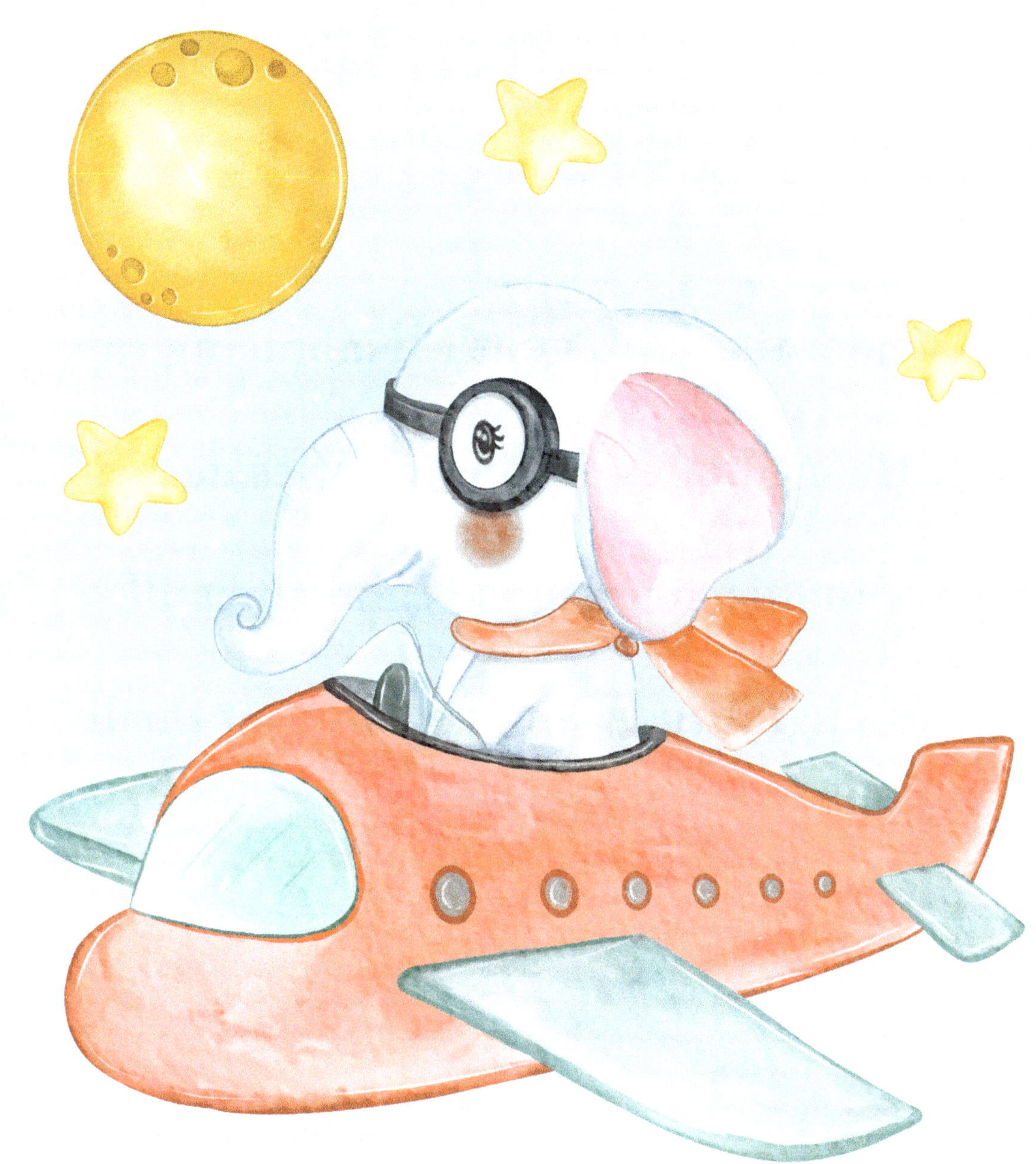

Under the sun's gentle, embracing ray,

He meditates, letting worries decay.

"In this moment, so calm and still,

I find gratitude, an ever-present thrill."

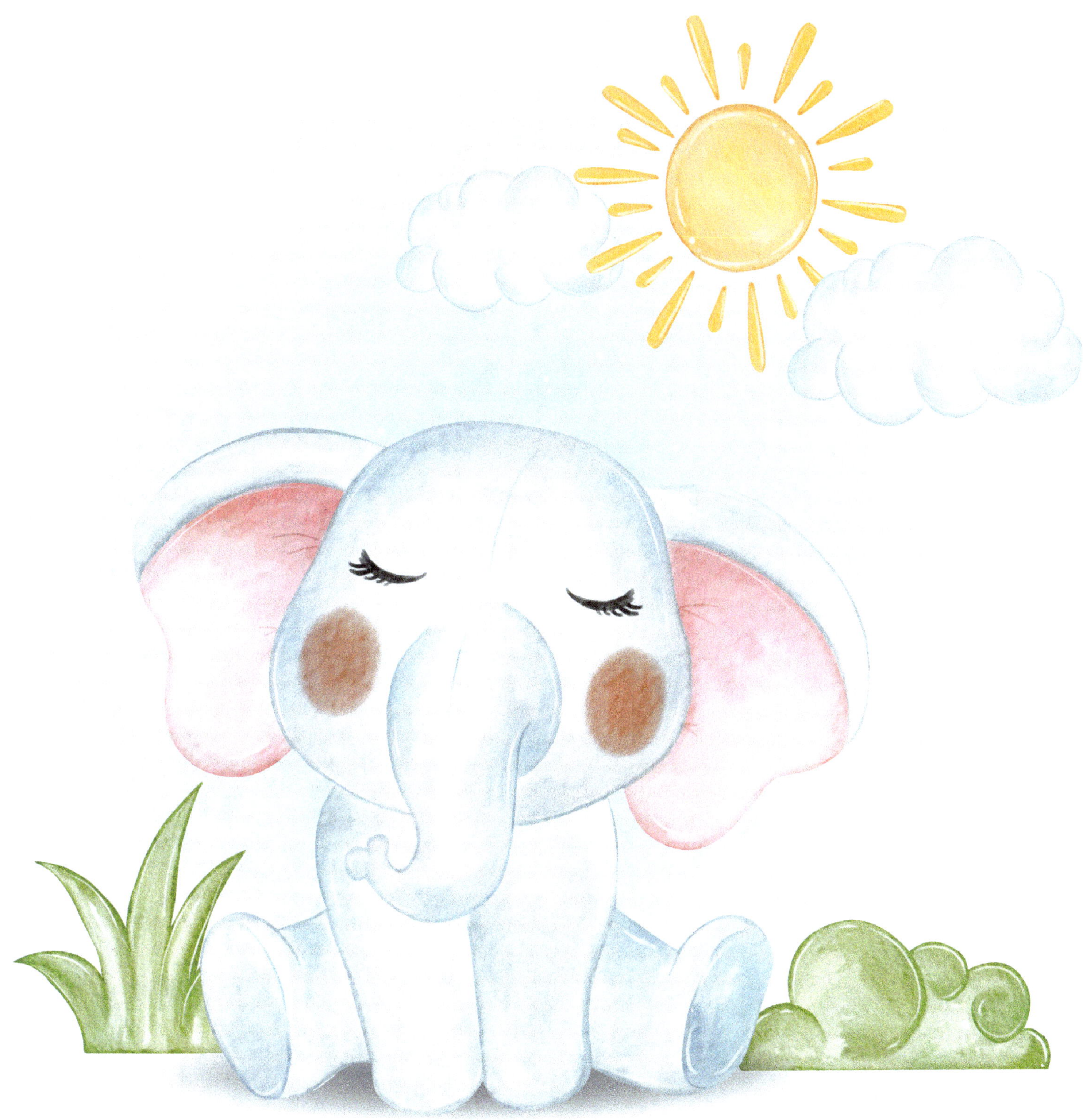

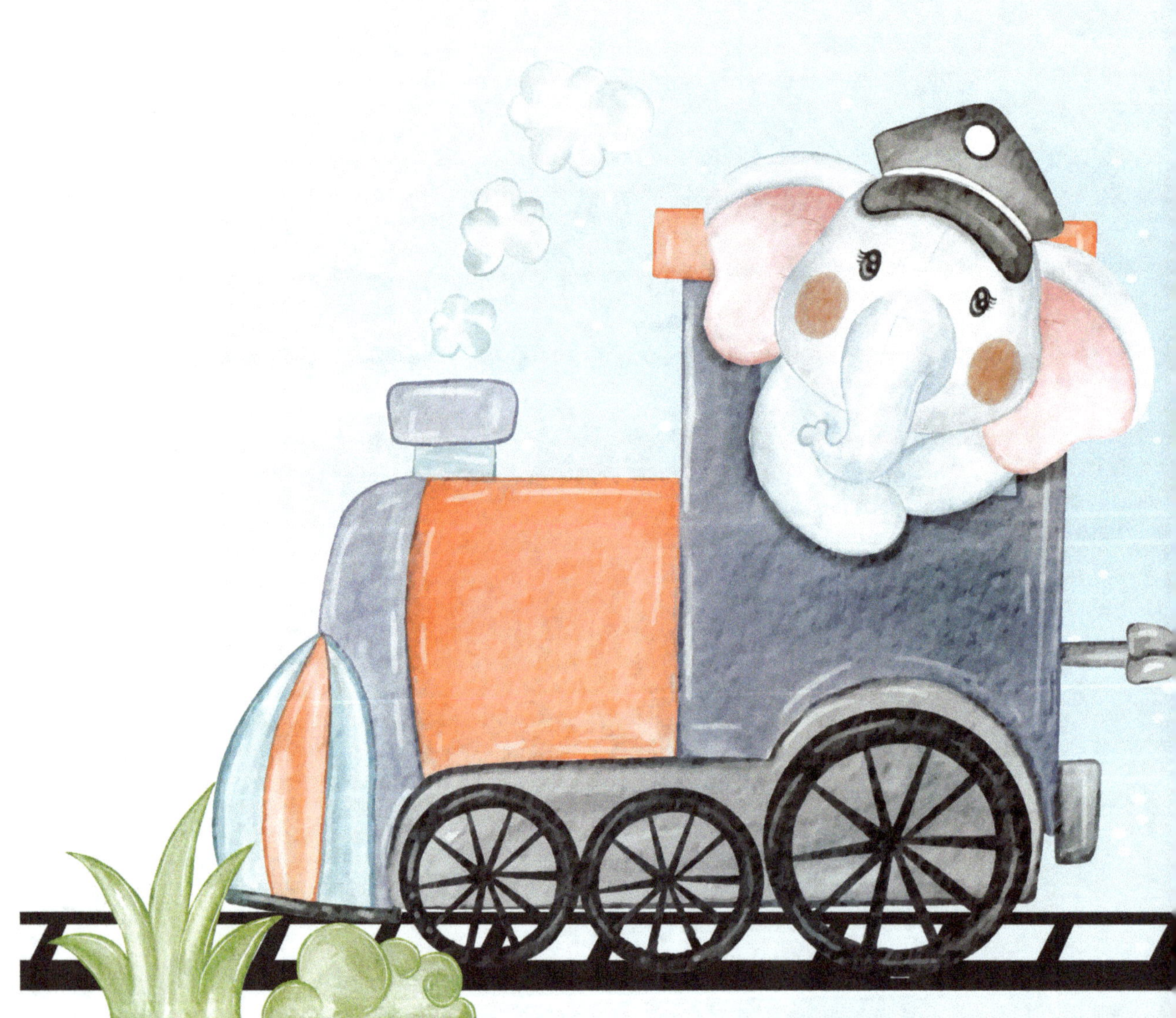

On a cart filled with treats,

so delightful and grand,

Zen Elephant shares with a giving hand.

"For bounty aplenty, I'm thankful indeed,

And sharing is truly the best way to proceed."

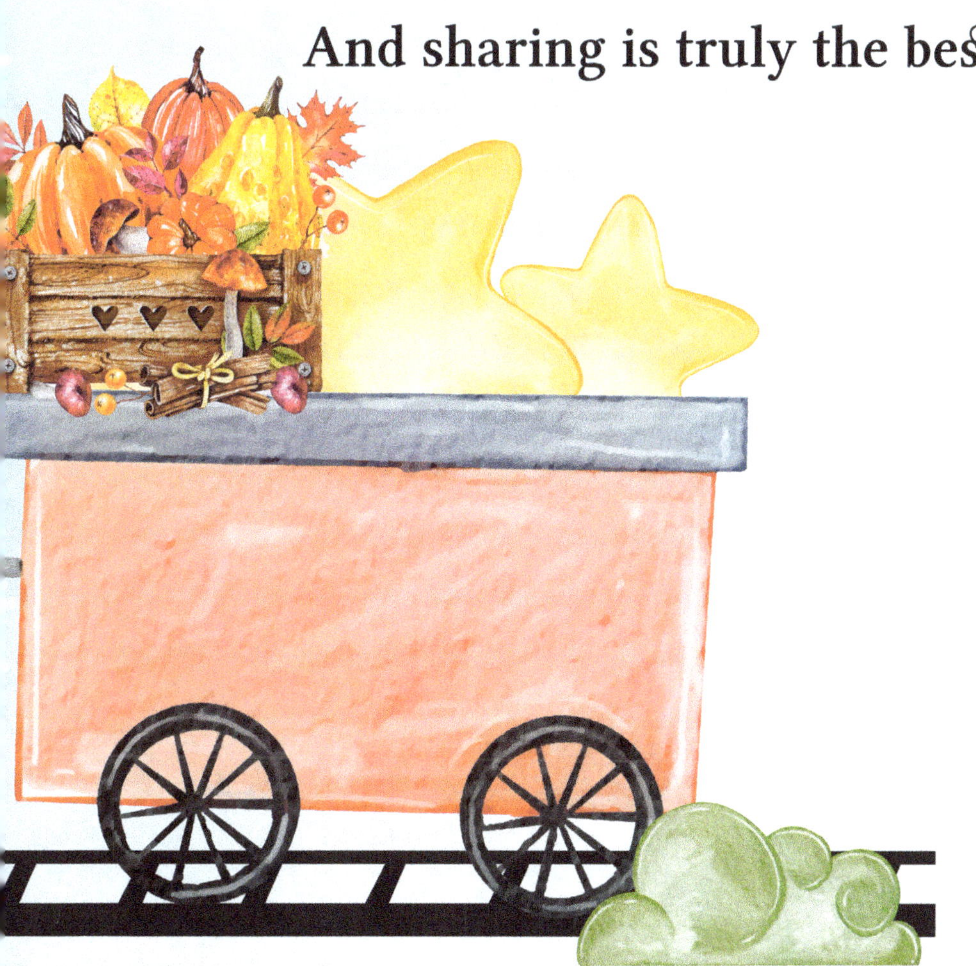

With a toy car, so small and so fun,

He plays, enjoying the run.

"Even in play, there's a lesson to find,

Be present, be joyful, and always be kind."

On a cart filled with treats,

so delightful and grand,

Zen Elephant shares with a giving hand.

"For bounty aplenty, I'm thankful indeed,

And sharing is truly the best way to proceed."

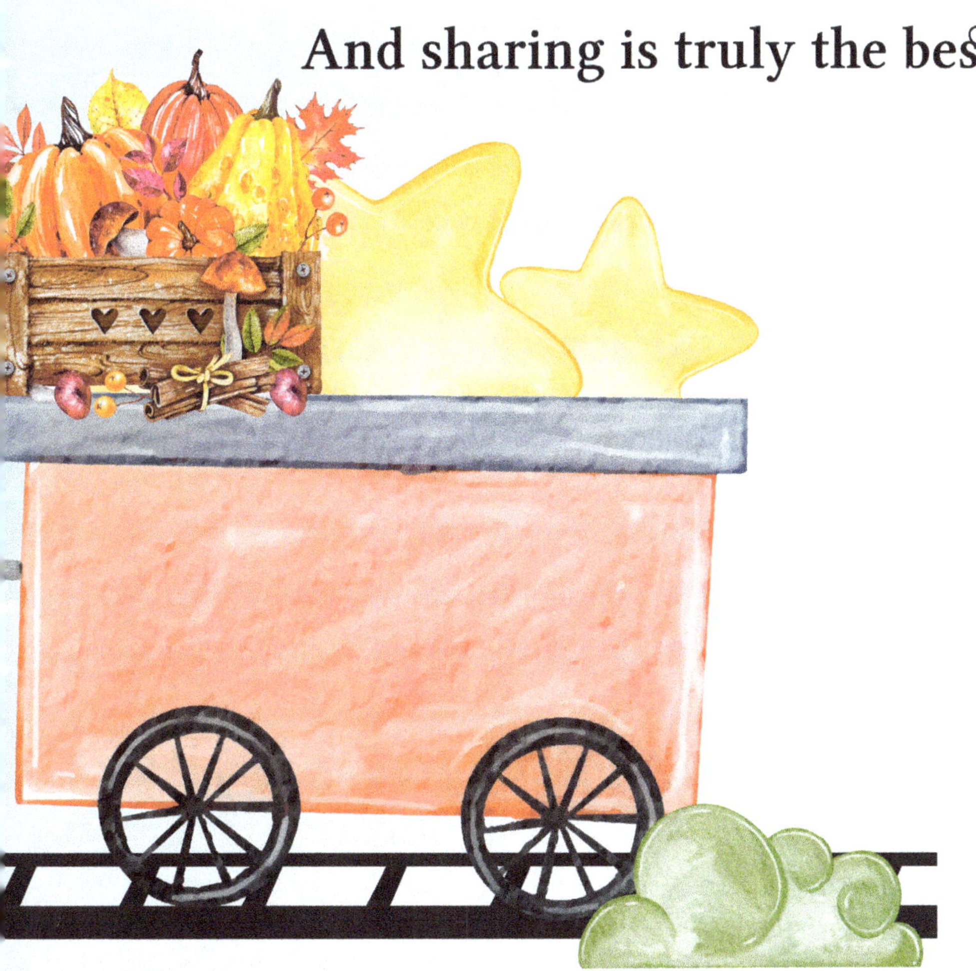

With a toy car, so small and so fun,

He plays, enjoying the run.

"Even in play, there's a lesson to find,

Be present, be joyful, and always be kind."

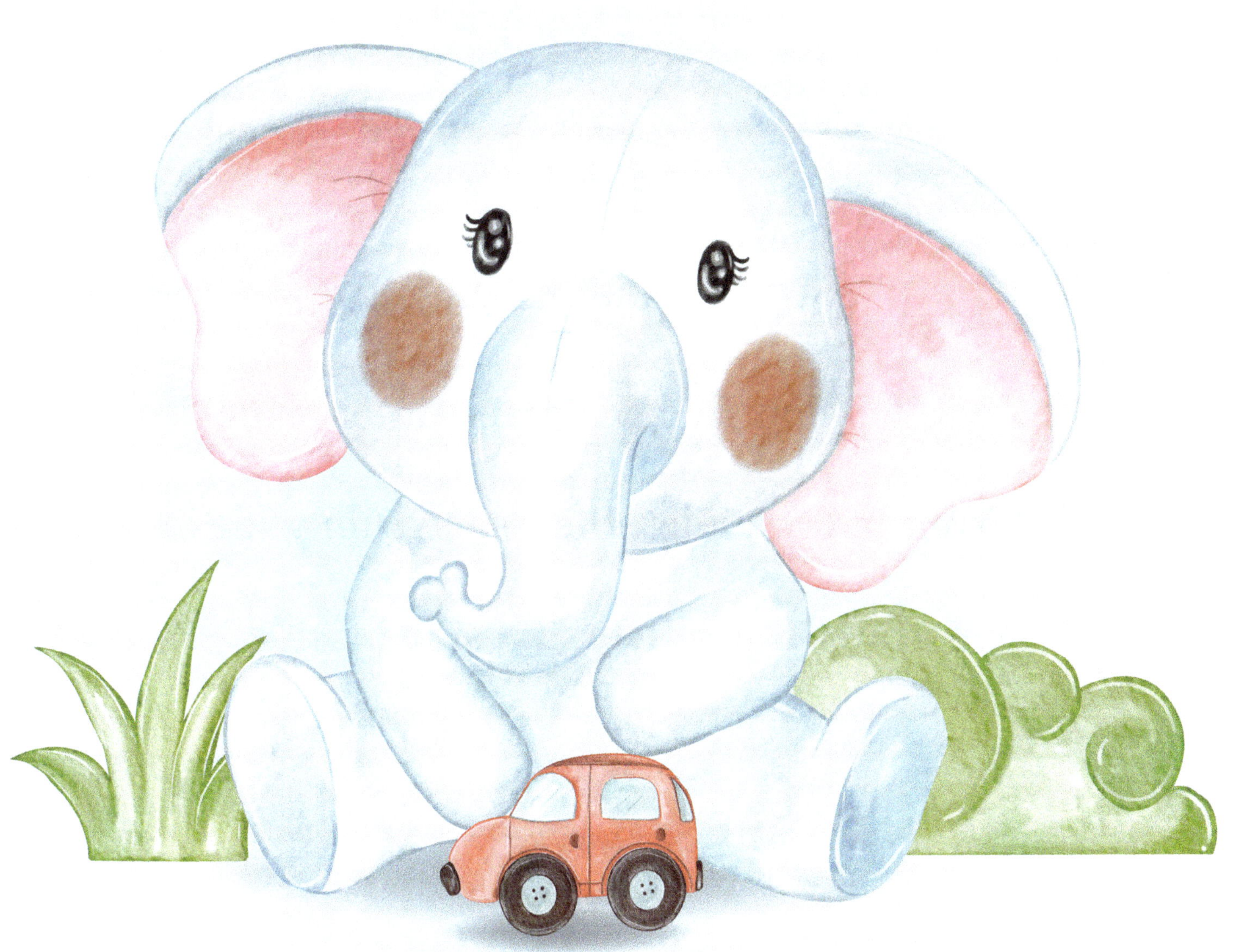

Resting on a rainbow, colors so fine,

Zen Elephant sleeps, dreams intertwine.

"From red to violet, life's spectrum wide,

I'm grateful for diversity, side by side."

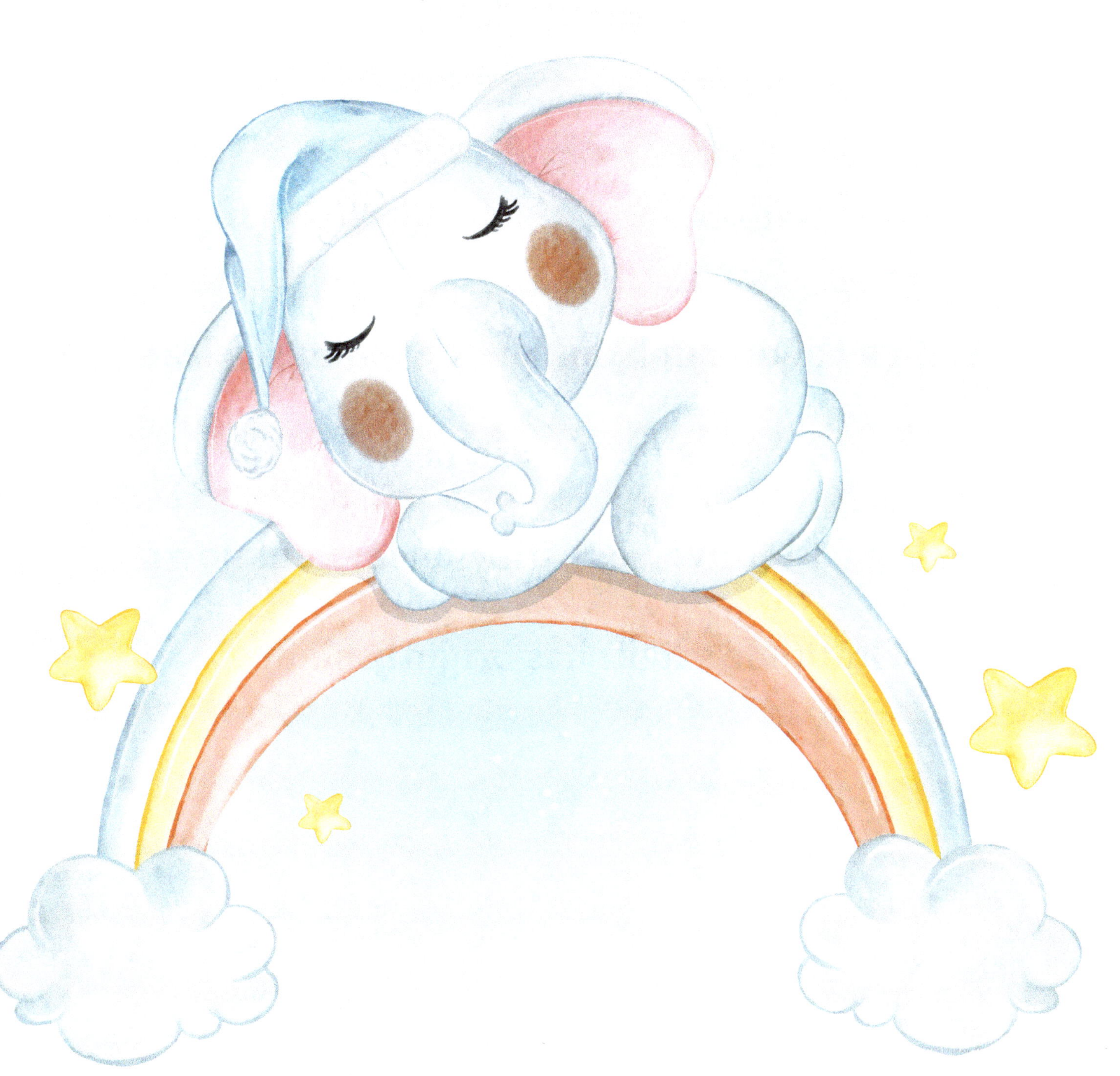

With a balloon in hand, on the moon so clear,

He sits, stars so near.

"In the vast universe, with wonders unknown,

Gratitude's light has brightly shone."

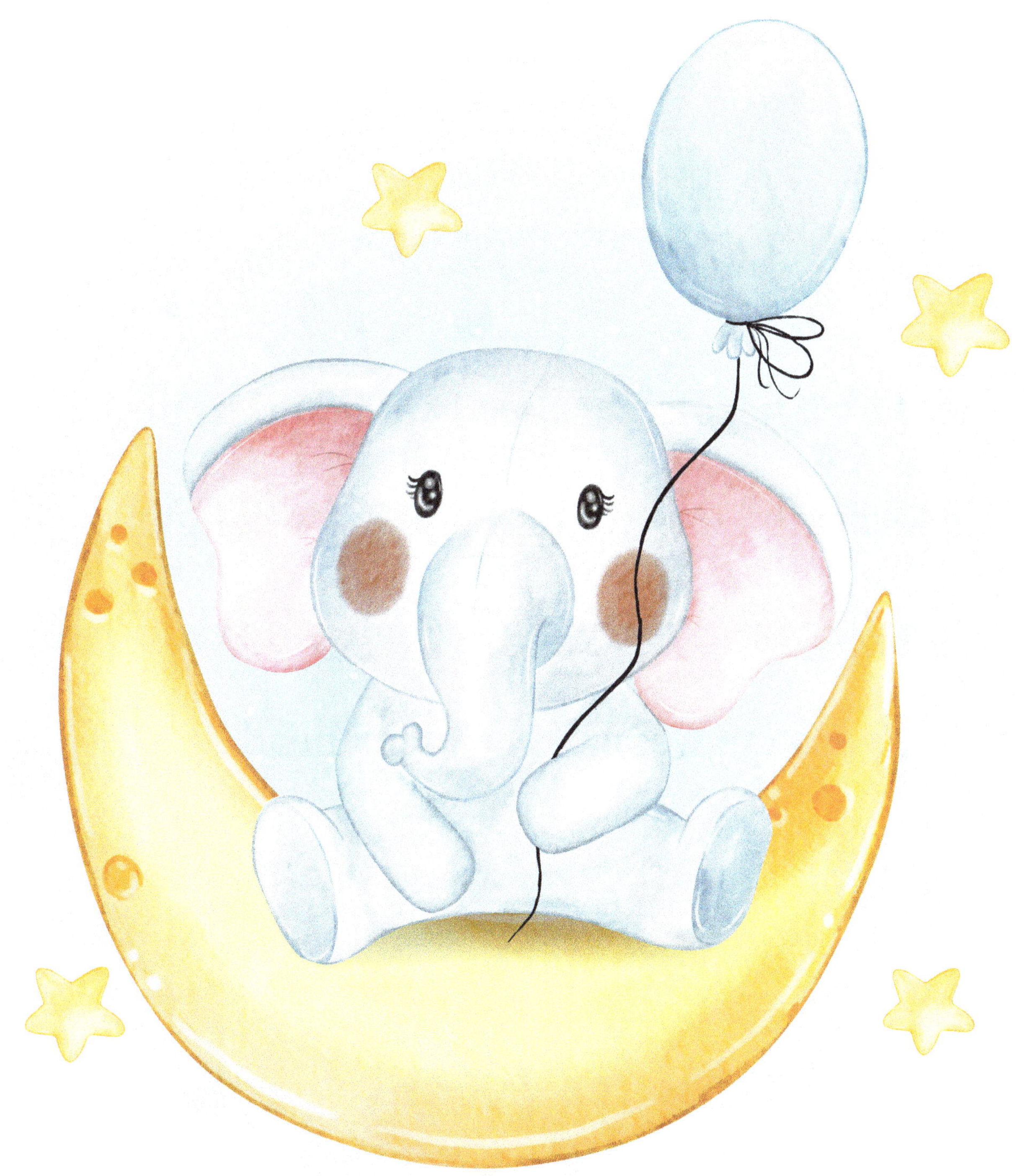

Held by a needle, wrapped snug and tight,

Underneath clouds, Zen Elephant's delight.

"Challenges arise, yet gratitude's thread,

Keeps me warm, keeps me ahead."

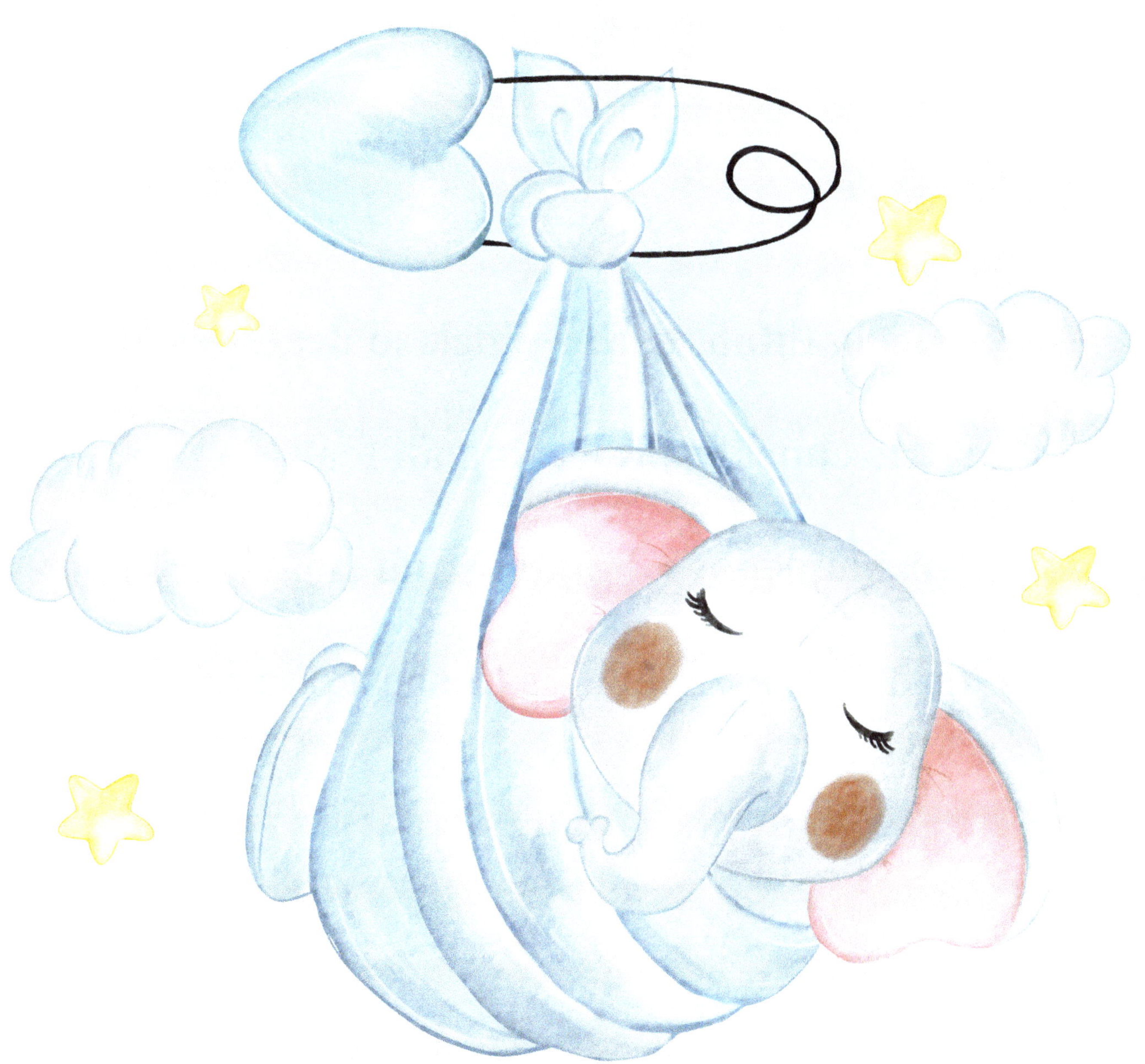

In a bathtub, with a chick so dear,

He chuckles, releasing all fear.

"In simple joys, both big and small,

Gratitude, my friend, is the best of all."

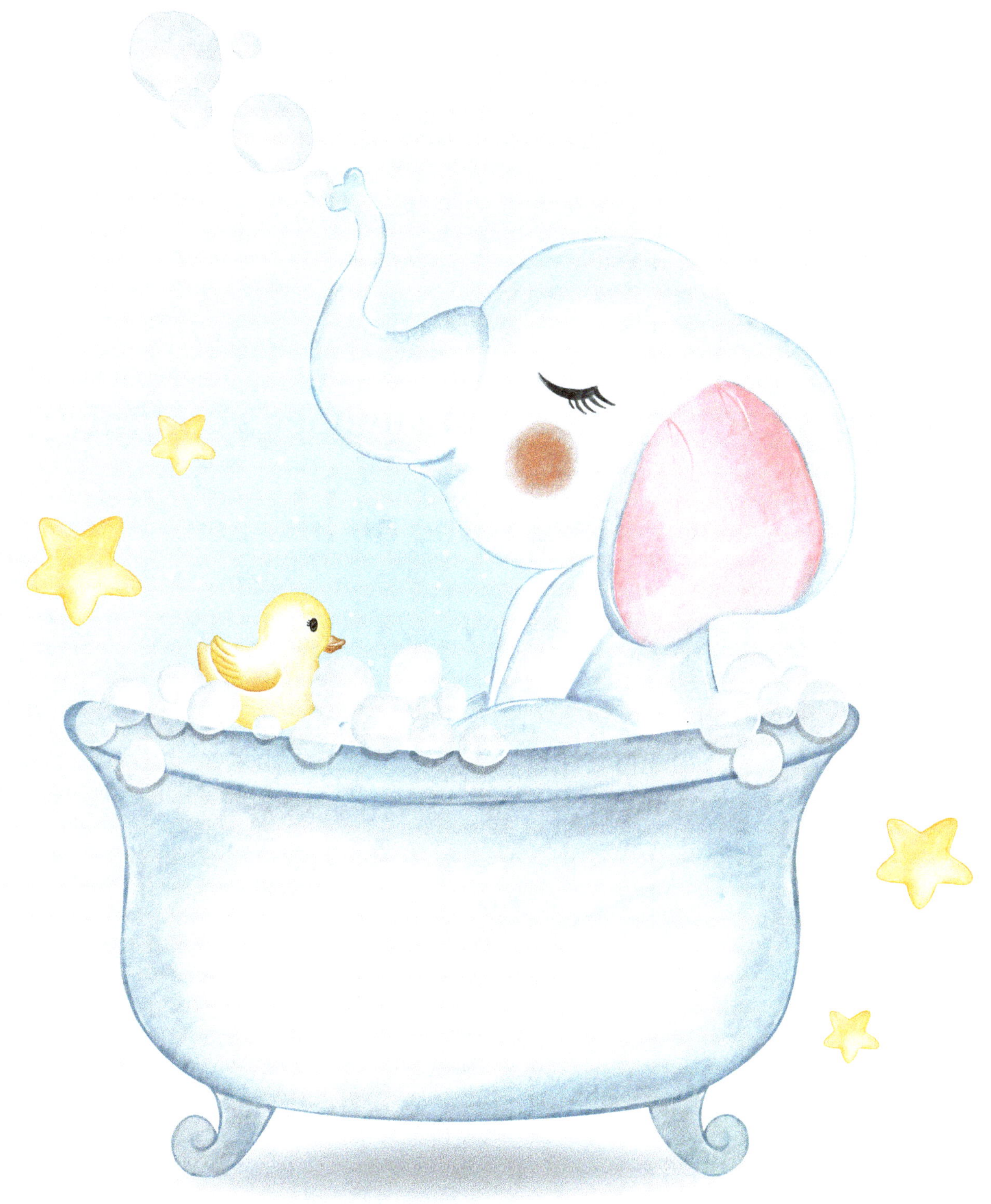

Beneath the cloud, in slumber's embrace,

He rests, a smile on his face.

"For days well spent and nights so sweet,

I'm thankful, from head to feet."

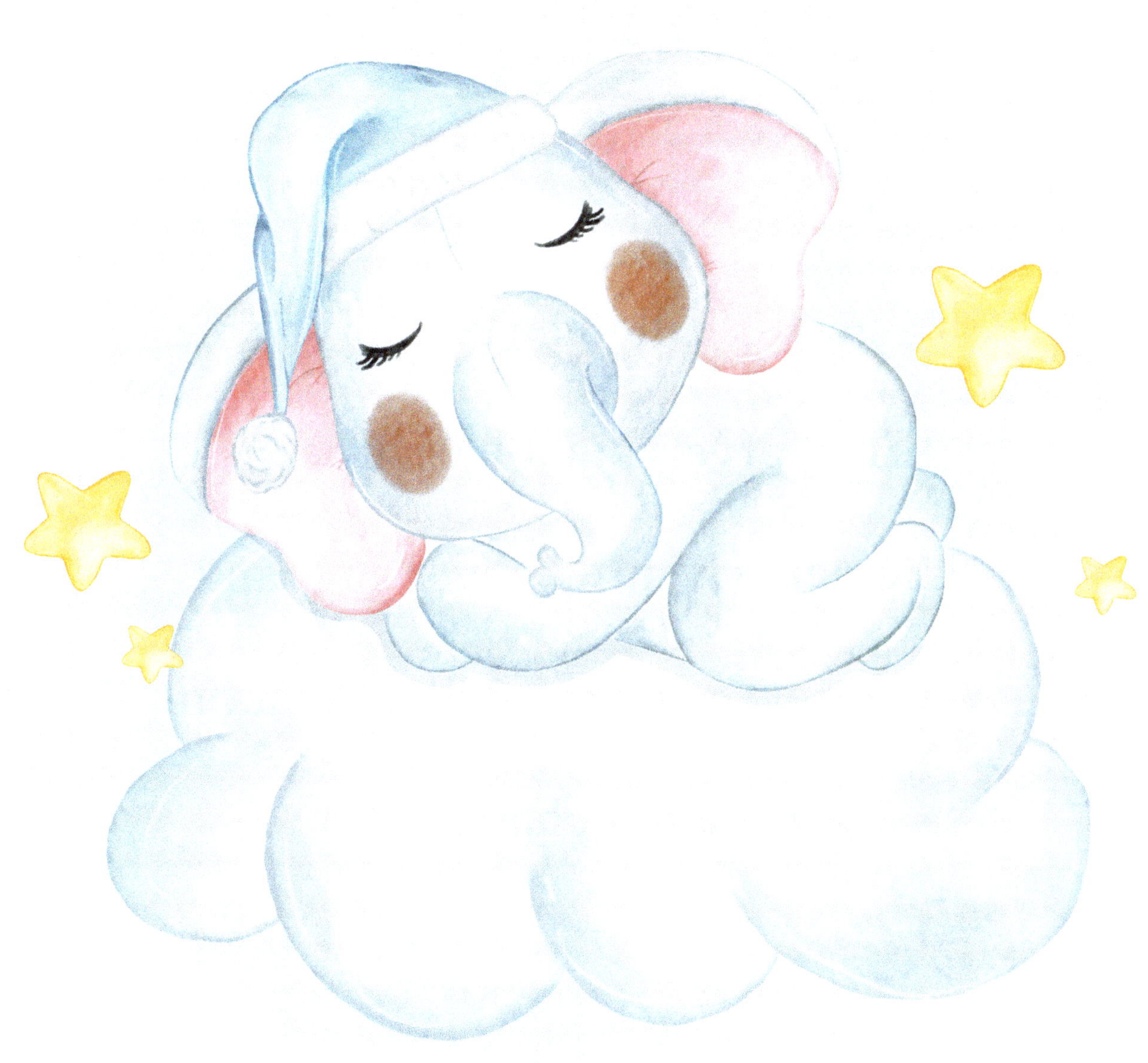

On a hot air balloon, floating so free,

He marvels at all he can see.

"Life's an adventure, ever so grand,

And for every moment, I'm thankful,

hand in hand."

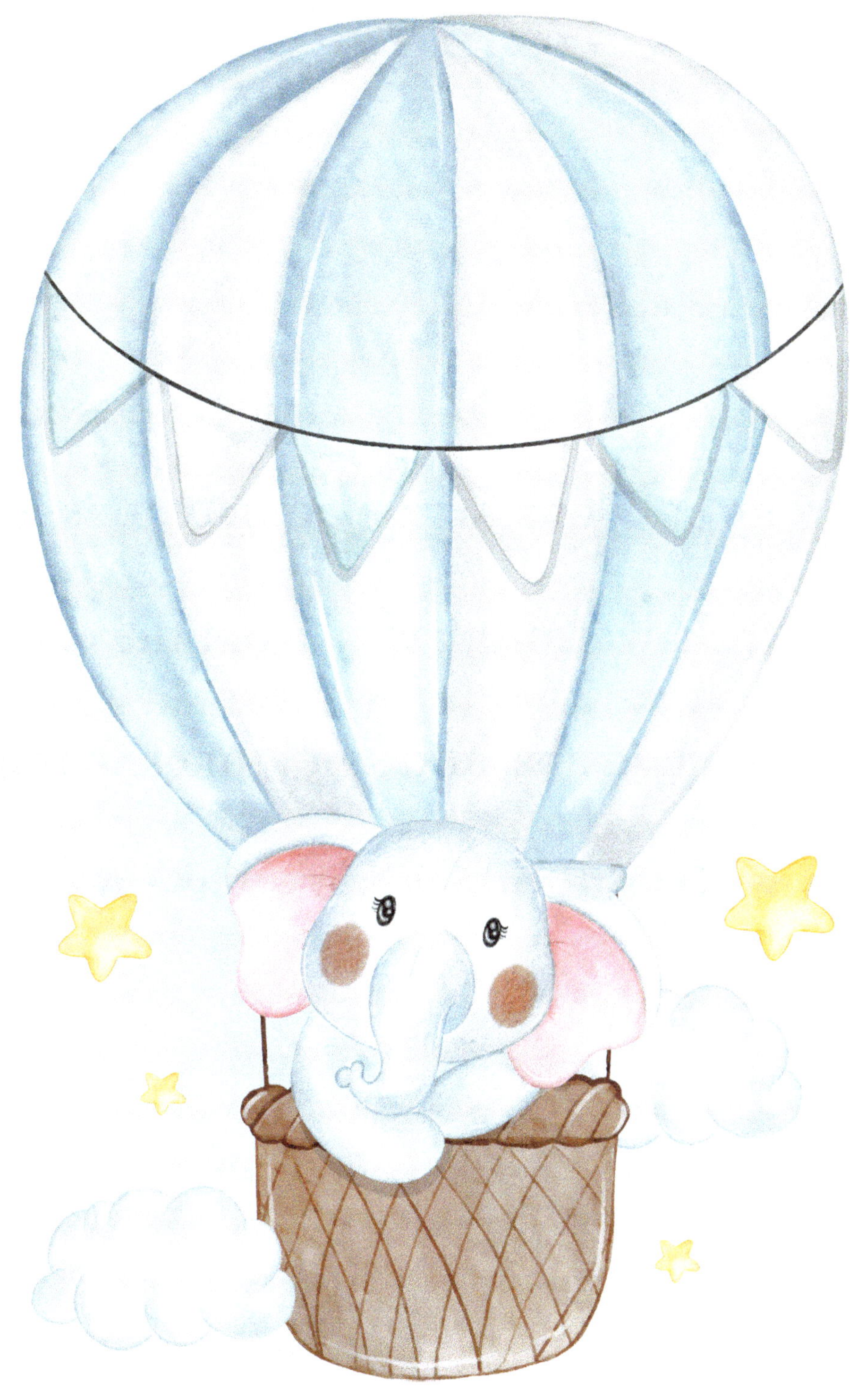

Held by balloons, wrapped in cloth's fold,

He feels warmth, away from the cold.

"Life may have ups, and sometimes it's rough,

But with gratitude, I know I'm enough."

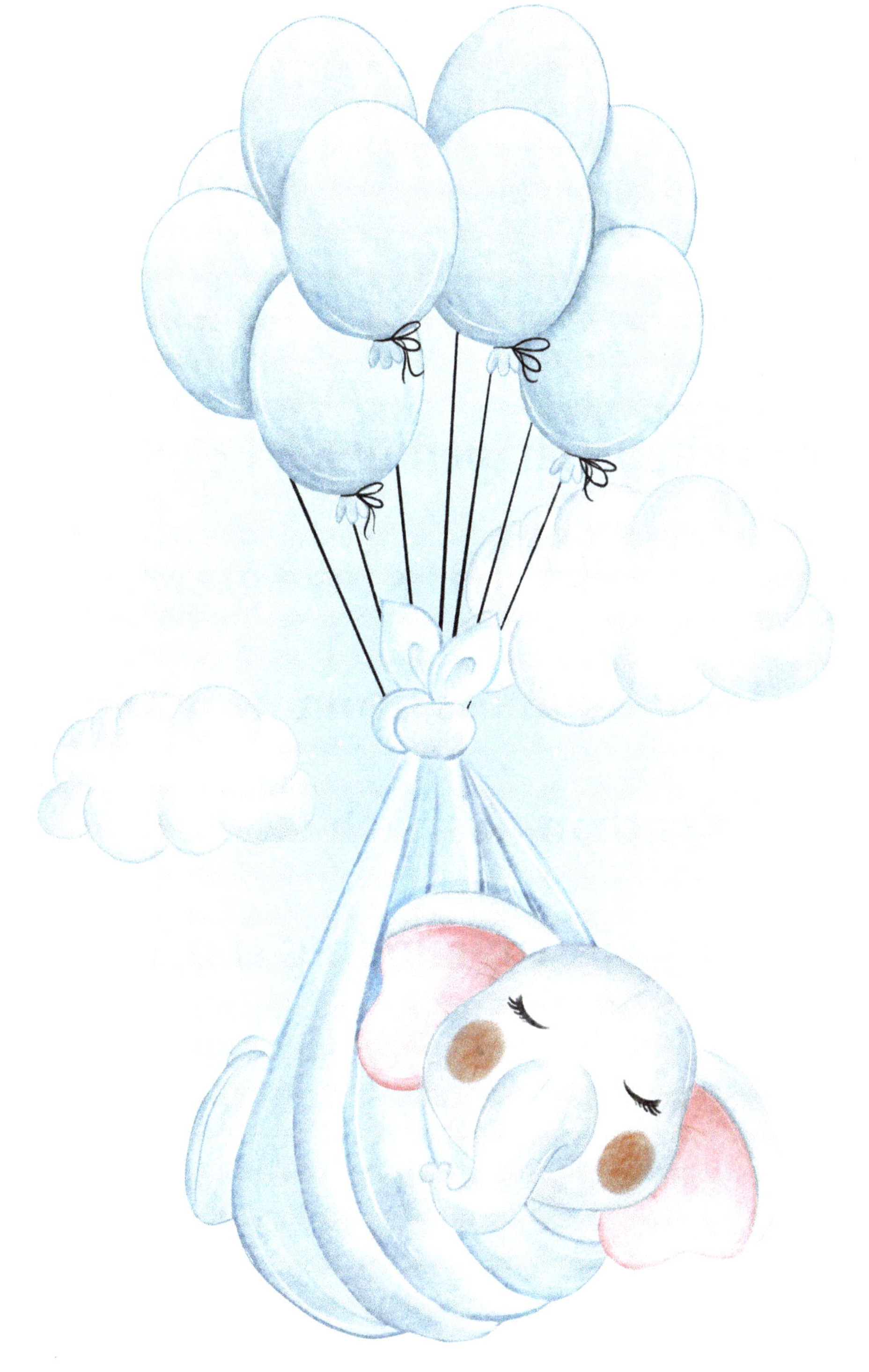

Holding a balloon shaped like a heart so true,

Under a cloud, His love grew.

"For love and kindness, from near and far,

I'm thankful each day,

for they're my guiding star."

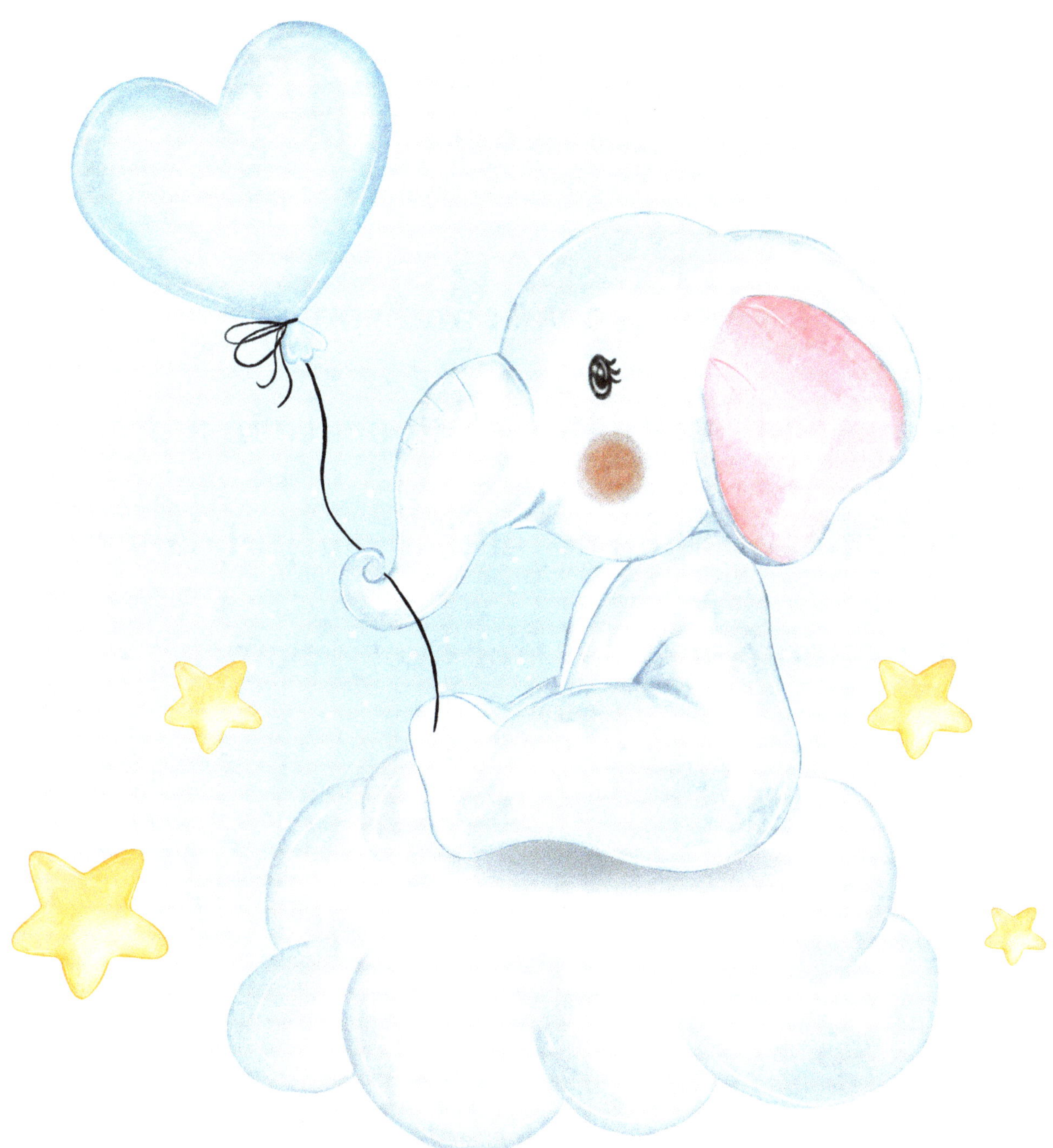

On the world, so vast and so wide,

Zen Elephant meditates, with peace inside.

"For this life, this journey, this beautiful dance,

I'm grateful each day, for every chance."

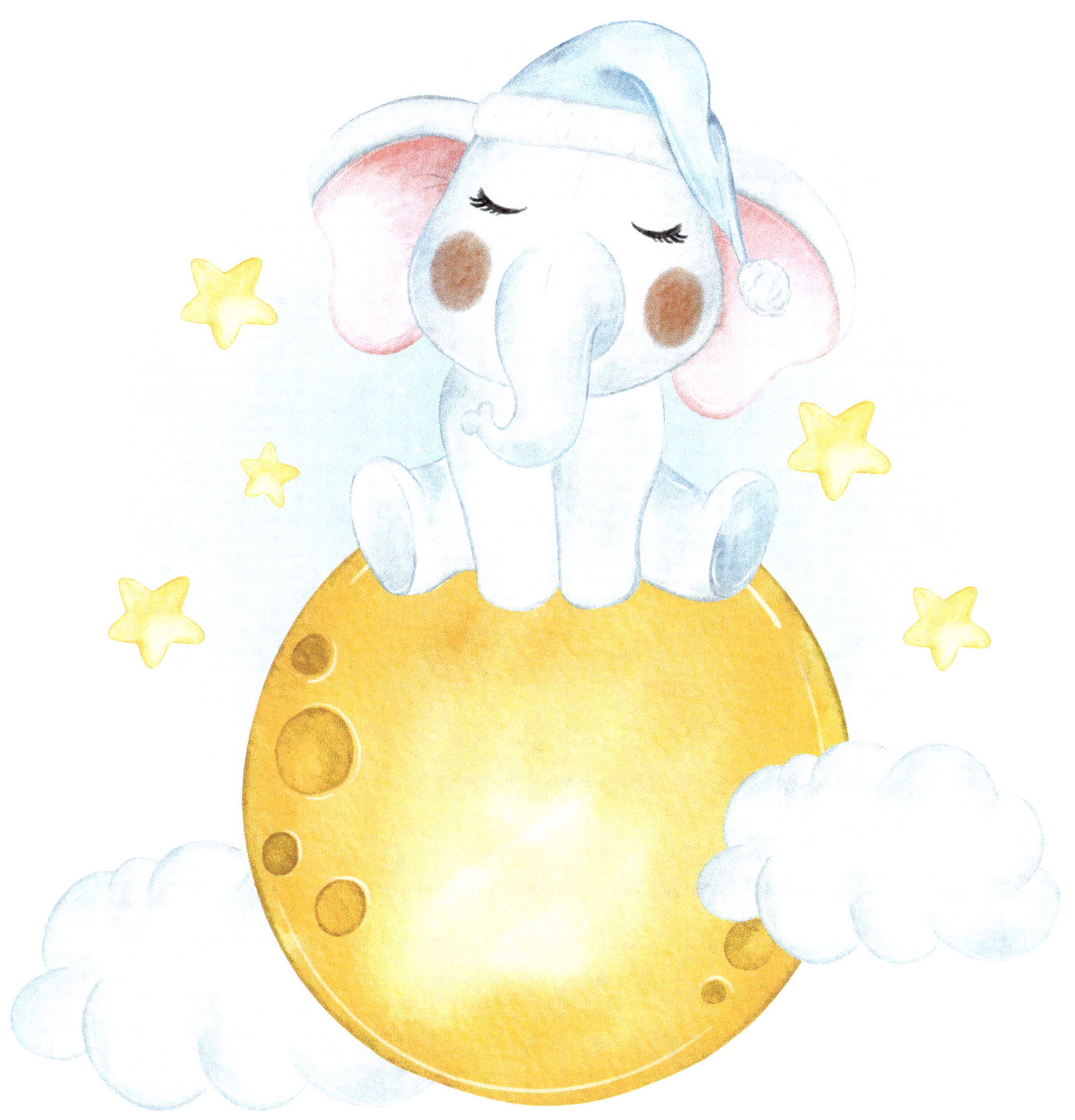

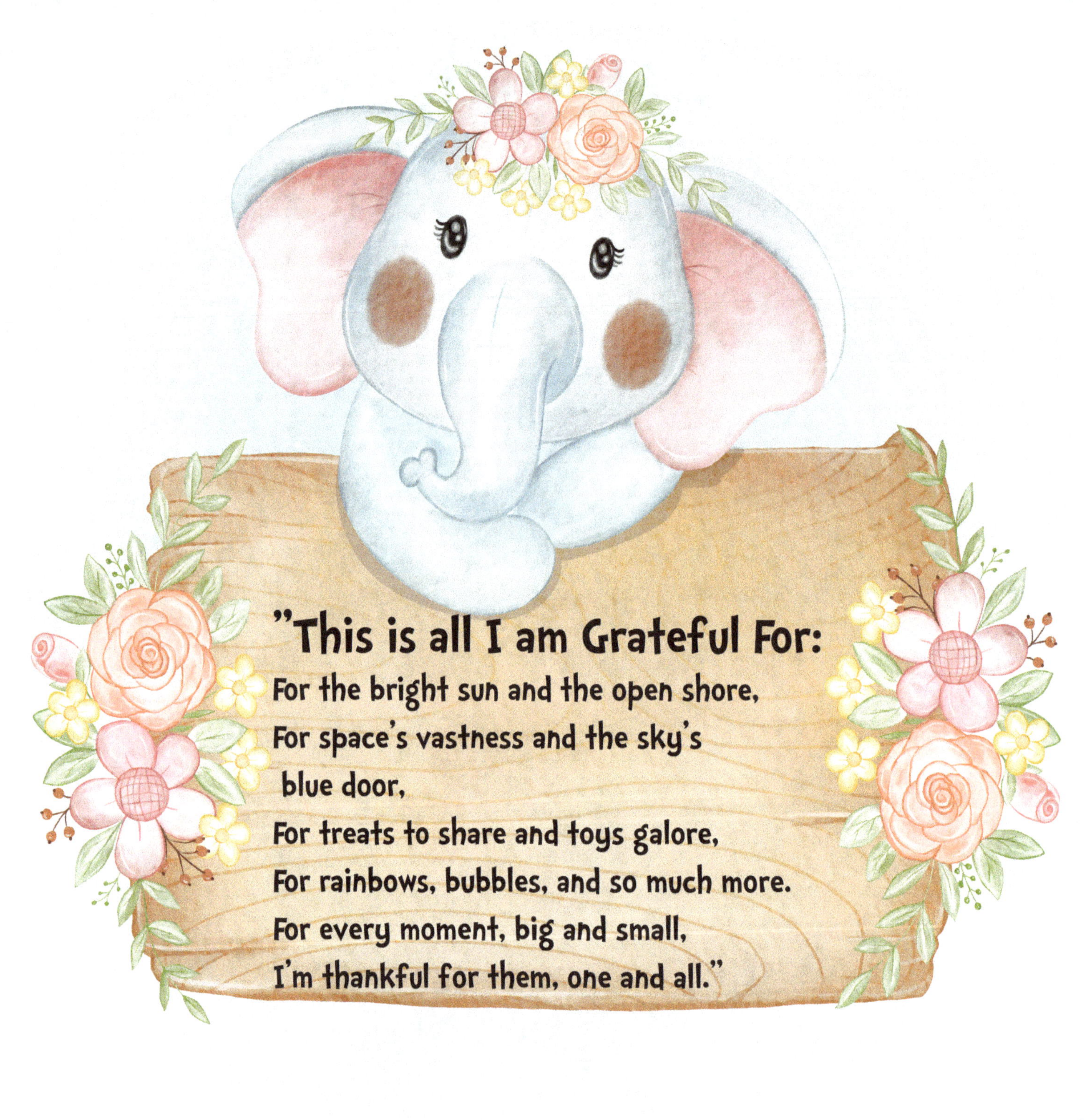

"This is all I am Grateful For:
For the bright sun and the open shore,
For space's vastness and the sky's
blue door,
For treats to share and toys galore,
For rainbows, bubbles, and so much more.
For every moment, big and small,
I'm thankful for them, one and all."

www.ingramcontent.com/pod-product-compliance
Lightning Source LLC
Chambersburg PA
CBHW081304130726

47998CB00010B/2923